Confessions of a Moonflower

Confessions of a Moonflower

Rebecca Fionna

authorHOUSE®

AuthorHouse™ UK
1663 Liberty Drive
Bloomington, IN 47403 USA
www.authorhouse.co.uk
Phone: 0800.197.4150

Published by AuthorHouse 10/26/2018

ISBN: 978-1-7283-8002-5 (sc)
ISBN: 978-1-7283-8001-8 (e)

Print information available on the last page.

Dedicated to Audrey C. Bartels
Thank you for believing in me when I didn't and for
encouraging me to cultivate my creativity since childhood.

Foreword

"Understanding is the first step to acceptance, and only with acceptance can there be recovery." — J.K. Rowling, "Harry Potter and the Goblet of Fire"

My goal with this book is to raise awareness for the neglectful way mental illness is approached not only in society but specifically in the realm of education. I hope that by raising awareness, universities may implement programs and resources where students may go for help and support as they actively try to find their diagnosis and a doctor that benefits them rather than just speaking with a token counselor.

I had untreated ADD and BPD (Borderline Personality Disorder) growing up which severely impacted my life. As a result, I struggled with confidence yet maintained an image of a normal girl who nobody suspected was suffering.

At first, I decided to write this book because, to be blunt, I did not want to live anymore, and I needed a way to externalize my suffering. My symptoms only intensified in my early twenties, as untreated symptoms naturally do. If I couldn't live for myself, I could live for this book. However, as I slowly healed and grew stronger, my goal for this book shifted from being just my therapy to being therapy for others. If I could find healing, I know others can too, and if being vulnerable and sharing my story helps make even one person feel less alone, I know my suffering was not in vain.

College Life

I did not have a normal college experience. Not only was I plagued with my undiagnosed symptoms, I was battered and sexually assaulted my sophomore year. For months after, I could not sleep or function with PTSD. In an effort to try to recover, I went to dozens of doctors, each one turning me away by saying things would improve with time, that I should change my diet, that I wasn't trying hard enough, or that since I looked fine I must be exaggerating.

This made me feel like there was something innately wrong with me as a human being which only intensified my symptoms. Eventually, I snapped, overdosed and was hospitalized. They misdiagnosed me with depression so I did not improve over a period of time which felt like a disappointment to my loved ones who all wanted to see me get better. Throughout this process, I was completely alone. Some friends at the time brushed off my cries for help by telling me that I needed to grow up, that I didn't have it so bad, and that it was inappropriate, selfish, and embarrassing to talk about my mental health needs. My inability to recover had me feeling like a burden not only to professionals but to my friends, some who told me I wasn't trying hard enough to heal. Little did they know how many doctors turned me away. In an effort to avoid my friends abandoning me, I isolated myself so I wouldn't disappoint them further. This only made my symptoms worse.

If I had resources at the university to support me while I searched for a doctor during this time, I know the process would have been less traumatic and I wouldn't have felt as much crippling shame each time I lost points from my grade from a panic attack keeping me away from class or from weeks of compromised sleep slowing my progress. I would have felt less alone knowing that other people experienced my symptoms. So when my social circle acted like my symptoms didn't exist and didn't matter, I believed them because nobody was telling me otherwise. I was truly alone, and felt like all my symptoms were personal flaws that didn't deserve attention because not even the ones who claimed to love me were validating them and were instead silencing me.

Despite these symptoms, I was one of the most motivated students in my undergraduate career. I was grateful for every class that I could attend without a panic attack keeping me away. Though I loved learning, my academic performance suffered and multiple professors referred to my writing as, "disappointing." My favorite professor during my sophomore year looked me in the eyes and told me I had a "serious problem with words" which completely crushed my spirit. I had another professor tell me that he was surprised my writing was so bad since I performed so well in the classroom. This negative feedback only contributed to my symptoms and their suffocating grip on my life. Why was I so bad at something I was so passionate about?

Since nobody believed me, I believed I must be crazy, a burden, stupid, and a monster. This was only intensified by how the professors I admired labeled my academic performance, which was the only thing that motivated me to leave bed in the morning, as "disappointing". In addition, the friends who belittled my trauma only made me feel more hopeless. I know now that I was not a disappointment. Rather, I was forced to live with mental disorders that nobody believed were real.

I hope that, if any students struggling with their mental health are holding this book,that you know you aren't alone and that you are fiercely intelligent and strong to still be in school despite your mental illness symptoms, especially with how little universities support mental health issues. I hope that you do not give up, that you fight for your mental health because as hard as it is to believe, it does get better once you find your diagnosis and a doctor that works for you. I hope that you know that you deserve respect and friends who honor your boundaries as you seek recovery.

Graduate School

After hospitalizations with no visitors, overdosing, and panic attacks so severe I couldn't speak, move, or breathe while my face turned blue, five years of hell became an MA in Medieval History, a high school dream come true. Yet, I couldn't excel because I was still suffering from untreated and unrecognized disorders which only worsened as I grew older.

At age 24 after years of invalidation and belittlement, I felt like an imposter in academia and life itself. I didn't know what illness I had and I couldn't provide the university's office of disabilities with documentation of my illness because I couldn't get treatment. Little did I know that BPD is not treated by all psychiatrists and therapists because it is stigmatized in the mental health community. I never heard of BPD at this point in my life and not knowing made the experience scarier. Campus counsellors couldn't help me since they were not equipped to treat me. I ended up using up all my sessions and still felt like I wanted to die.

My motivation to learn kept me going. I did my best but my best was not enough as my grades suffered. Like in college, professors told me my work was disappointing and sent me away without any positive feedback or advice on how to improve. I was drowning but nothing could be done. I needed a diagnosis.

Finally, I became frantic one day and made an appointment with a seemingly friendly looking lady on ZocDoc. The same day, I went into her office and tried to tell her my symptoms in a nervous mess, bracing myself for the usual doctor response of belittlement. I was shaking, crying on and off, and I couldn't even engage in eye contact.

But for once when it came to doctors, I was lucky. She actually diagnosed me with the correct illnesses. Through her treatment specializing in CBT (Cognitive Behavioral Therapy) and DBT (Dialectical Behavioral Therapy), I improved along with my grades and social life. Not only did I learn what BPD was and that I have it, I learned that BPD is shunned by many psychiatrists and therapists because it's stigmatized in the mental health community. Many believe that this is incurable or people with BPD are a waste of time. Now I understood why so many doctors told me they wouldn't treat me due to my symptoms being "too severe".

Yet, here I am, proving them wrong with my healing and with this book. I am living proof that with proper therapeutic and psychiatric care along with a motivated spirit, managing BPD is possible. It's my dream that symptoms of mental illness will be normalized instead of taboo, and that universities will support students who are fighting mental illness. It is also my hope that universities will implement programs for mental health support so that students may find safe places to speak about symptoms. But most importantly, I hope that by reading this book, anyone who struggles from mental illness feels less alone.

Here lie the wild
Flowers of my fractured soul,
Grown from plots of 12 pt.
Times New Roman soil.

Contents

Fight

She buried her vulnerability
And it bloomed into armor.

-Warrior

I don't write for people to like me.
I write for people just like me.

-*Purpose*

Throw your hands up
Let the ashes fall like rain
From every bridge you ever burned

-And dance

If you aren't interested
In learning my secrets,
Then why are you
Lecturing me
About them?

-I have my own thoughts, don't you know?

She is drowning.
Her friends watch,
Blaming her for
Being too weak
To swim.

-Some currents are invisible

I forgive you
But I don't want you back.

-Consequences

You didn't expect
I'd lock you in
The same walls you built
To keep me out.

I opened my heart for you
But I never promised
The inside wasn't
A mess.

-If you don't like it, please don't come back

Introversion is not a personal flaw.

-I am not rejecting you, I just need to be alone for a while

Don't feed me poison
Then tell me I am
Toxic.

Dear men,
Telling me, "Not all men are bad"
Doesn't make me feel more safe
From the ones who are.

-My fear is not the thing that is the problem

This is not
A Trigger warning.

Because the kids
Who watched their friends

Die in homeroom
Never got one.

-Wake up

After all this time,
You were just in love
With your reflection
Sculpted by my words.

Every time I've been a victim,
I've been told
I love to play one.

-Me too

You think that
I don't want to be close
But the truth is
You are drunk by breakfast
And remember none
Of our conversations.

-Projection

Waiting for you is like
Waiting for an empty room
To breathe.

-Pointless

I'm stuck at
The bottom of this well
So tell me:
How does yelling at me
For falling
Help me climb out?

-Beating a dead horse

Every night,
I fight the same demons
That scared away so many
Who called themselves friends.

-And that makes me stronger than them

I spoke while
you plugged your ears.
Accusing me of hiding secrets
You didn't want
To hear.

-Mixed messages

I have been the shelter.
I have also been
The storm.

-Polarities

I'm an open book
But not everyone knows
How to read me.

-They don't take the time to learn

If you have
No good intentions
Why say you miss me?

I hate that they say
Borderlines are like burn unit victims,
That every touch on our skin is agony.

I hate that they say that because it's true.
I spend most of my time in a self-made
Astronaut suit cold enough to burn myself
And those who come too close.

And when they realize being around me is
Too hot, that it takes effort to make me feel safe,
They leave.

And whatever degree of burns they recieve
Will never compare to the pile of ash they
Leave behind.

The pile of ash is me.

-Please don't tell me you will stay if you're just going to leave.

You would rather
Call me crazy
Than admit you
Hurt my feelings.

-Scapegoat

Stop muting your voice
So that others are more comfortable.

-Speak

I've been through Hell
So often that my demons
Made me fireproof.

-Phoenix

I wondered how you saw
Everyone's pain except mine.
I didn't know to my pain you were
Colorblind.

-Invisible

You waited until
I developed the confidence
To trust you with my issues
Before you blamed me for them.

-Manipulative

You don't get to decide
Whether you hurt me or not
Or how much
Or in what ways
It's not up to you to say
It's my fault
For being too sensitive
And that I'm exaggerating.

-If you care, take the responsibility.

Not understanding my feelings
Doesn't make them any
Less real.

-Misunderstood

The stardust from your skin is blurry now
From bad memories slicing their visions
Into my astral-plane mercilessly.

-My wounds reopen easily

I hate crying.
And for once, I wanted to scream
Louder than a storm.
But my silence was already
Thunder.

There was no room for my feelings
In your narrative
So I grew a spine and attached to it
All the pages you left out.

They will try to burn you
To illuminate themselves by the light
Of your flames.

-Some pyromaniacs are never identified

Flight

Liquid gold
Seeps through her pores
Extracting sweetness from chaos.

-The heart of a beehive

If I can't rise with the sun
I will rise with the moon.

-Moonflower

I'm too busy dreaming
To be sleeping.

-Insomniac

I am not feisty
For having an opinion.

-Even if I'm wearing lingerie and stilettos

You deserve someone
Who appreciates the
Otherworldly magic
Within your veins.

-Don't settle for less

Ignite everything you touch.

-Unapologetically

Don't think that
Just because I'm pretty
Means you can walk all
Over me.

-Try and I'll slice your legs off

They say she went mad
But really
She just didn't care about
Their opinions anymore.

-The day she became a dangerous woman

My dreams are
More realistic
Than your promises,
Darling.

Your kiss
Brings on psychosis.

-In a good way

Sometimes I'm not sure
If I'm on a diet from life or death.

Sticks and stones
        Never broke my bones
But careless words
        Made them pop up
Like Daisies.

-Words hurt

I seek darkness
So that I may tip toe
On starlight.

-Not afraid of the dark

Falling in love with him would have her
Fall out of love with love.

-She's just another lost coin in the wishing well

Treat me like
A delicate flower
And touch me like
A meteor shower.

-Dichotomies

You can measure a man's confidence
By how much he is threatened
By yours.

-A confident man will not be threatened by a woman's power

I'm no criminal
But too many men
Chase me as if there was a price
On my head.

-Wanted not loved

They call me
"The skinny bitch"
And I smile,
Keeping secret that
Even skinny bitches have
Minds that can be
Overweight with insecurities
Just like anyone else.

-And they say they look perfect on me

The dirt
Made me who I am
So it's fine if you drag
My name through it.

-It'll just make me stronger

She smoked cigarettes
Knowing the smoke was the tunnel
Her demons walked to enter
Her lungs.

-She'd rather have them keep her company than be alone

I could be
More angry at you
But I'm no angel, either.

I love the way
You always find the light
Even in the darkness
Of my eyes.

-My candle

I know what you never told me.
I just didn't say anything because I was
Curious to see if you'd be honest.

-Who played who?

Freeze

Emotions are neighborhoods
I find myself lost in without the memory
Of the streets I walked to get there.

-Sleep walker

Another day
Another rich
Celebrity joking
that they
Have a
Split personality
Because they
Like to
Use drugs
and read
I wonder
If they
Would glamorize
A split
Personality if
They met
Someone who
Actually is
Diagnosed but
Isn't rich
And instead
Is shunned
By society
Like me
They probably
Would still
Joke anyway
I mean
Look at
Marilyn Monroe
Rumor has
It she
Had a
Split personality

But nobody
Talks about
Her suicide
Without glamour
And sex
And I
Wonder how
She would
Feel hearing
Famous people
Exploit the
Mentally ill
Just to
Appear more
Mysteriously sexy
But what's
The use
Wondering that
She's dead
And there's
A chance
One day
I'll die
The same
Way and
The famous
Will still
Joke about
Split personalities
To draw
Attention long
After I'm
Cold in
The ground.

-*Exploited*

A stream flows over rocks,
Trying to reclaim its waveless
Reflection.

-Like me

Her eyes drip blue ink
Staining her glass skin
With the depths of her own
Humanity.

I'm at the bottom of the ocean
But I don't feel any pressure.

-Novocaine

As if between mirrors I see you;
an alleyway of replicas
competing for your reflection.

-Which one is you?

She cut herself
Too deep with the edges
Of her shattered heart.

Do you know what it's like
To watch words leave your mouth
That were never yours?

-Puppet

Sometimes I climb up
The tree of isolation
So high I can't see
The way down.

-Stuck

We swallow our secrets
Until they grow large enough
To eat us.

-From the inside out

Our memories fell like
Petals from my snowy heart
Until none of us
Was left for spring.

-The winter that killed us

Avoiding mirrors,
So I don't have to
See the face of my
Mistakes.

-On the run from myself

Does hope
Show you signs when there are none;
Phantoms in between notes;
Ghosts outlined in sage smoke?

What is real?
I'm a posing porcelain doll,
Wearing expressions you want to see.

-Not all actresses are in Hollywood

Now I know
How Rapunzel feels.
Locked in her tower,
Measuring her age
By the length
Of her
Hair.

-Trapped

My bottled up feelings
For you ran out of ink.

-Finally empty

Spiderlike,
I spin silver to catch feelings
That taste like my image in mirrors.

-Reflectionless

Pills fly towards my hospital gown
Like flowers that follow the sun.

-Treatment

Raindrops on the car window
Are destined to slide to the same
Inevitable destination- together
And alone.

Depression is a dream
Where my face is a lake;
Even when light shines on it,
It remains expressionless.

-Frozen

Just because I'm
Too anxious to speak
Doesn't mean I don't have
Things to say.

-*Quiet not stupid*

Submit

I'm sorry
That sometimes my mental
MIllness wins.

-I wish I could have been stronger

I never saw
A shadow in you
I could not love.

If actions speak
Louder than words
Then why is it
So silent?

I hide from you between bedsheets
But my own nails catch the fabric
Folding into the shape
Of your face.

New bed sheets
High thread count
New silk nightgown
Strapping me in the middle of the bed
Between you and bricks
I thought I could write
Out of the wall of my brain
With poetry
But the words dropped me
In the cold Atlantic sea
Swimming to your island
Your metal neglect
Weighs down on me
The waves carry your laughter as
I open my mouth for air but
Water floods my lungs instead
I wake up coughing
Out a soccer ball
I dribble it across your field
Sprinting to you but I fall
Mud in my mouth
Dirt under my fingernails
I plant flowers there
Hoping they grow into balloons
To float me away from here
Between you and cold bricks
In the middle of the bed.

I have learned
To love your absence.
It has always been closer
To me than you.

-Neglect

Sometimes I go underwater so that
I don't have to feel the tears
Streaming down my face.

-*Mermaid*

I cut out my spine
When I decided to give you up.

-The only thing that ever held me up

How can you tell me:
                I don't take time to talk to you
                When you don't create time
                                For me to take?

I keep eating dark chocolate
Its darkness reminds me of you...
How I would keep the bitterness
You left me with rather than
None of you.

-Cravings

Waterfalls of stars
Fall from my eyes,
Staining your photograph.

I just want
To listen to sad music
And drink wine tonight.

Sometimes
I am so sad
I cannot write.

-There is nothing poetic about despair

I feel myself tumbling again
Down a train of thought
I assume I got over
Years ago
When the hospital staff
Led me to the sun
And to my smile
As I learned
To believe
In God
But here I am
Falling down a red
Waterfall, counting the drops
Like rose petals as I search for hope
Within wickedness that spins my
Truths into fictions and my
Body into a propeller
That nobody can
Catch.

-Relapse

I guess you can't make
Any mistakes if you've already
Given up.

I want to escape
From my story.
From who I am.
From my past.
From my heart
And who it has
Loved and lost.
I want to escape
To forget everything
That hurt me.

-The only story I can't close is my own

Do you remember
When we were a harmony
Not a dissonance?

-The music changes when promises are broken

Ruby's fall from my broken heart,
A fortune that you will never have.

-The value of a bleeding heart

Before you,
I did not know words
Could splinter bones.

When I shrink,
You grow tall.
Filling up my spaces
Until there's nothing left
Of me at all.

-Feeding on my insecurities

We orbit each other
Like birds set on fire
Doomed to never touch
One another.

My fear is
Friends and family
Forgetting my name:
Depression and I
Sound almost
The same.

Suffering is a painting
Society stares at
Hands in pockets
Saying nothing
Doing nothing
Just watching and judging
It's quality of entertainment
Before something else
Catches its attention.

I'm sorry that sometimes
I fall from my skin to hide
Inside the marrow of my bones
And ask you to find me like
Thunder without lightning.

-Dissociation

I just want to stay in bed
And listen to the
Rain today.

Some things are still too raw
To write about.

-Don't rush me, I'm healing

I'm glad you could
Move on so fast
Because I'm still just
A walking mess you made
And never cleaned.

Attach

Here's to another day
Hoping you'll choose me
As your favorite Pokemon.

You make
Angels from
My monsters.

-Master chemist

It wasn't logical.
But it made sense.
-Us

You are like
The aroma of coffee,
Warm comfort coaxing me awake
A bittersweet kiss I would trade in
Dreams to taste.

Your touch turns my skin
Into a navy sky that we lay under
To count the stars at night.

-Cosmic

My skin dissolves
Into rose petals wherever
He touches.

I feel safe
In the company
Of your monsters.

-They make me feel normal

Your fingers trace my collarbone
As if to study the way to holds my heart
Together.

-Kinesthetics

Your eyes
Burn through my atoms
Leaving graffiti on
My DNA.

-Irrevocable

A reluctant butterfly
Clings to its cocoon
Afraid to fly from the place
That created its wings.

-Darkness feels safer sometimes

It only took texting you
In my tiny NYC apartment room
To fall madly in love with you.

-A little goes a long way

I blush
Just thinking about
The poems I could
Write for you.

I don't need you to
Understand me
I just need you
To try.

-All I ask

Even the ocean
Holds up a mirror
To catch the shimmer
From the stars in your eyes.

-You are cosmic

Pull me close
Like the moon
Pulls the sea.

-Even from thousands of miles away

Your imagination
Is a deluge of
Angelic fire.

Your love is
The only fire
That does not
Burn.

Those stars in your eyes
Collapsed into black holes
Of irresistible gravity.

-And now I am falling

Forgetting you
Was like asking the heart
To forget its rhythm,
Asking the stars to forget
How to burn.

-Unnatural

I just wanted to plant flowers with you.
But you kept stomping on our seeds.

-Why didn't you give us a chance?

He is reliable and gentle
Like the dawn.

-You are my sunshine

Detach

She folds her heartbreak
Like origami
Transforming oceans
Into teardrops.

Loneliness is my oasis
I'll send you a postcard of me
Rolling in my king-sized bed.

-Solitude is *my favorite vacation*

Forgetting feels like forever
And remembering is
A river that always
Dries up on itself.

-Time travel

What a curious torment it is
To peer through the cracks of
Your mind's crumbling walls.

-Out of body

Some call themselves mermaids
Hoping they will not drown in the sea
Of mortality.

-Humanity

Depression is a hurricane
A barrier between me and the sunshine
I know exists above the clouds.

-Wait out the storm

I loved him
Like I loved the stars.
I knew I'd never touch
Them either.

I thought only the moon
Could shed its own light
Until one day, nobody
Could see me too.

-I can make myself disappear

My love fills books
That he will never read.

Heal

She dreams of a love
That drowns oceans

I have seen
A miracle's signature
Written in her scars.

-They spell: survivor

There's this secret fire
Inside a woman's heart
It incinerates all monsters
Who try to lock us
In the dark.

-Resilience

Her heart
Even had Satan
Wish he was still
An angel.

-Heavenly

Learning how to understand
Each other's silence is just as
Important as understanding
Each other's words.

When winter
Runs through her veins
She is not afraid,
Choosing instead to
Marvel at the way
Winter always brightens
The stars.

-*Perspective*

She found herself
Angry at the sea
For encouraging her
To let go after
Each wave.

-It's okay to be angry

It's easier
To believe
The negative
Things you
Think they
Think about
You, right?

-Don't fall for your own tricks

No matter how harsh
Winter comes and leaves,
Spring still blooms.

-Despite it all

I can love myself
And know that I need to change.
A seed cannot rise above the dirt
Until it breaks.

-Trust the process

Even lonely stars
Still shine.

I like to imagine
That flowers bloom
And hummingbirds sing
In the abandoned ruins
Of our love.

-For they are still beautiful and precious to me

Until you touched me, I was a shadow.

-You brought me back to life

Rip out the weeds
From your heart to make
Room for flowers to bloom.

*-Don't think that you don't deserve more
sunshine because you do*

My grandmother didn't die.
An angel just asked her to dance.

-She said yes

Birds sing, picking up dead twigs
To build a home for new life.

-Spring

You may not be here
But your silver-blue magic
Wraps me in a frozen halo
And If I dance at a certain angle,
I catch the shadow from your rings,
Falling upon my sun kissed skin.

-Now I understand why Saturn dances

Pain is like the wind.
You breathe it in and breathe
Out fire powerful enough
To burn down nations.

-*Dragons*

So many men
Are like Icarus.

Flying too close
With beeswax wings.

And when they melt,
They blame me for
Burning too bright,

Forgetting that I am the sun.

-And the sun doesn't apologize to anyone

It's okay
If your "better days"
Are still a little grey.

-You're doing great

Yes,
I still may be fighting my demons.

-But don't think for a second I can't defeat them